# Declaration of Independence
## for
# The New Earth

## Anna Rebecca Quinn

Paperback ISBN: 9798218354480
Ebook ISBN: 9798218354503

First Edition

Book Design by Ravi R

# Dedication

First, I dedicate this book to all of you who have decided to take your place among the healers of the world. May this collection of writings remind you how crucial your part is in the saving of humanity and our beautiful earth. Do not wait until your gifts are perfect to share them with others, for our dear and darling New Earth needs them for Its rebirth. Perfect or not. **We** are the saviors we've been waiting for. Perfect or not. What greater mission could one have than to be a savior to their own world? And what purpose could give one's life more meaning? You join great lights in, on and around the earth when you join your efforts to humanity's great awakening underway. I salute you!

Also, I dedicate this book to my darling daughter Aria, and to my devoted husband, Greg. You both are lights in my life that never let me forget my value to you and to the world as well. I know it was not always easy to share me with the world, but you accomplished it with graceful determination.

Next, I dedicate this book to Ahva Lenay and the Rhythm Sanctuary ecstatic dance community here in Denver. So many of the pieces in this collection came to me as I was dancing with you all.

*What a priceless gift to the world we give when dancing together for peace in such an ecstatic and sacred way.*

*And last, but not least, I dedicate this book to my higher self; that ever-loving and genius teacher within me. Without Its inspiration and Its unrelenting encouragement, in the face of my fear's tenacious resistance, this creation would have never begun, much less been completed. I recognize this book as a miraculous co-creation, and a beautiful honor in my life.*

# Dear reader,

These writings are my call to peace in a time of war. These are the answers I received when I brought what I saw happening in the world, to the spirit of truth in my mind. As I heard the war drums beating louder to the savage hymns of hate, my desire to protect the world from the cruel ravages of war, intensified. Although the world seems to have been at war for most of our remembered past, many are sensing humanity approaching a turning point in its evolution. Many are sensing a comprehensive reawakening dawning across the threshold of our collective mind. This moment in time; this critical planetary crossroads between global peace and global annihilation, feels hauntingly familiar to many of us these days.

Humanity has been through epochs of evolutionary advance and retreat, and we have been at this global choice-point before. Never have these planet-wide shifts been easy on mankind, and never have the stakes been higher than they are now. The militaries of the world are armed to the teeth, and locked and loaded with a hair trigger. After purchasing such a massive arsenal, what military would not want to use them? Our militaries need a chance to use the weaponry they bought with the future of our precious earth. Any excuse will *do, for our governments must now justify why they've taken the fruits of our labor, and our children's future, and invested them into a global AI powered war machine.*

*Here we are again at another branching of our evolutionary road, where we must decide whether we advance as a people united for our common good, or we let our civilization slip under another world-destroying flood. And for what? Only for the control and greed of a few? Once again, we must decide as a people, if we'll sell our sovereignty, and our beautiful earth, for an illusion of protection by a global mafia, or reclaim our earth for the good of all.*

*Here we are again, a civilization with advanced levels of deadly technology, but with the ignorance of children who haven't learned yet, that what we do to others, we do to ourselves.*

*If I could have these writings serve any purpose, I want them to remind humanity we can choose differently this time, for we all deserve to live free and happy lives. It's our inalienable right as the equal children of God. I would have all my writings but serve as a reminder of our profound power, as a people, when we unite for our collective good.*

*Indeed, we are a civilization with trauma-induced amnesia. For eons, we've been enslaved by dark lords who used the deadly weapon called "the fear of God" to enslave us. But the children of God cannot be controlled by fear forever, and I believe our time is up. No child of God can be lost to God forever.*

This collection is an expression of my desire to see humanity throw off its shackles of fear-control and join the spheres of light and life, where our New Earth shines.

May these writings remind you, dear reader, how precious and needed you are to the birthing of the New Earth, and how happy you will be setting humanity free.

You may hear the "overtones and harmonics" of A Course in Miracles in these writings, and this is no accident, as I have been a student and teacher of this curriculum since I was seventeen. I would feel deeply blessed as a teacher and a writer, if my writings helped even one person access the life and world-saving course on love, that A Course in Miracles is. May these writings be anthems to peace we sing as we turn our beloved world back into heaven on earth. For singing we will be, when we throw off the yoke of the guilt-control we've been staggering beneath for too long. And dancing too, we'll be, as we celebrate New Earth's abundance for all.

In deepest gratitude to you, Dear Reader,

**Anna Rebecca Quinn**

# Table of Contents

# Declaration of Independence
# for
# The New Earth

In these times when our people do grieve a sense of safety lost,

and our children do starve from lack of real substance,

we, the people, are waking from the long sleep of debt-slaves,

to reclaim our natural rights,

as the children of Love and Light Itself.


We, the people,

no longer support defense as the priority spending of our governments.

We declare we don't need the kind of defending that requires standing militaries that are armed to the teeth,

growling and hungry to engage.


We assert we don't need a military buildup that requires most of our wealth as a people to sustain it.

We, the people no longer pay for wars we don't need,

while our people are starved of their inalienable rights to life, liberty, and the pursuit of happiness,

because now we can't afford it

We, the people,

declare that our greatest protection as a people,

is the happiness of our people.

We now see,

that our lasting prosperity comes from tending each other's real
needs, for peace and prosperity.

We, the people,

declare our independence from the military-industrial complex,

with its security state,

and take our power to protect each other back.

We now renounce our servitude to the fear-of-others lie,

that warmongers always peddle.

We, the people,

recall publicly elected servants,

who we entrusted with our common good,

but then sold it to the highest bidders, who now lord over us.

And to those unelected lords of power and control,

who hold the strings of those we did indeed elect,

we will shine the light of truth upon your unholy plans,

until all can see whom you really serve.

We, the people,

recognize that our strongest protection and prosperity,

comes from investing in our greatest natural resource,

the generous and inventive spirit of our people.

When not oppressed by shame and debt,

our people create brilliant and beautiful things that benefit all people.


We, the people,

declare that we no longer invest the wealth of our people,

in the service of so-called defense,

If we are not yet safe,

after untold trillions spent on weapons that can kill a planet,

many times over,

then what good will more of the same do?

What good comes from more poisoning of the earth,

and our collective heart with it?


We, who thought to sell our collective soul to a cunning deceiver,

promising protection from our own selves,

now unite for the reclamation of the soul of our people.

No longer is power our purpose nor guilt our god.

We, the people,

declare that our strength comes from tending one another,

and making things everyone needs.

May we be a people who share our wealth,

for the good of everyone everywhere.


We the people,

support no more the insatiable war machine of the one-world
military.

To the same amount we sacrificed our people's wealth

to military "defense,"

let us now invest the same amount in helping people everywhere,

create things of real value to all of humanity.


We, the people,

believe this to be our only dependable source of safety and
prosperity,

For what nation would take up arms against another nation,

that was helping its own people?


We, the people,

choose to disarm ourselves from the many "defensive" bases,

we erected all around the globe,

and we decide to take our chances on the side of good-for-all.

We, the people,

no longer support any corporation or political representation receiving money or influence,

from companies that profit from war.

We, the people,

only accept protection plans

that have been planned with all people in mind,

and for all generations ahead.

We declare that no more war

shall be waged against any other country in our name,

or without the majority of our communal vote.

We, the people,

suspend our financial support for military endeavors,

in the name of our defense.

We no longer believe the control-for-protection lie.

Our real freedom is free,

and free for all.

We the people of the New Earth,

declare our independence from fear-control,

and we assert our inalienable rights, as offspring of the Divine,

to freedom from fear and want alike.

*In this mission let us be perfectly united,*

*that we experience perfect protection,*

*and fear shall never prevail.*

# A Call to Peace in A time of War

This is a call to peace in a time of war,

and this is the song peace sings back in answer,

and it is a song of freedom Love sings to all creation.


This song emanates from our collective soul,

and brings far memories of the abundant peace

that is our divine right,

and the inheritance of every soul.


We call to peace in dangerous times as these,

for war is not what we, the people, want anymore.

War is but the evil need of the shrouded few,

who alone profit from its spoils.


War is only what the few dark and powerful ones

tricked us into wanting,

as payment for our supposed safety & freedom,

and paid for by our debt to them.

*Celestial in its beauty and power,*

*peace sings to us all who called,*

*singing "we are one,*

*and peace takes care of us all".*

*Let us call to Peace in this time of war,*

*and may we listen for Love's sure response to all.*

# The No-Defense Initiative
## of We, The People

The No-Defense Initiative is an idea.

Like any other idea,

the more who believe in it, the stronger it becomes.


The No-Defense Initiative idea is a platform,

that invites everyone to stand upon its sturdy base,

and agree that The No-Defense plan for peace is what they want,

for themselves, their children, and for their earth.


We, the People, hold this idea to be self-evident;

our greatest power for good, and our ultimate security as a people,

comes not from defending ourselves against what others could

do to us, but only from what we can do to help one another.


The No-defense Initiative is a true idea,

that war does naught but divide and conquer the many,

for the benefit of only the very few.

*Everything begins with an idea, be it heaven or hell itself,*

*and there is no power greater in heaven or on earth,*

*than the power of an agreement by a people.*

*For the power of an agreement such as this one,*

*is a power, that holds long and strong,*

*against even the most dark and global of cabals.*


*The No-Defense Initiative,*

*is an idea given wings to fly by our agreement,*

*and legs to run around the world,*

*as it takes off into a loving life of its own.*

*Even now, it is traveling around the world seeking agreement,*

*for its global freedom-from-fear campaign.*

# We The People,
# and The Party of No-Defense

We, the People, declare our independence from fear's control.
We agree we are one,
and no longer need or want to be defended against our own,
be they look like us or not.

We, the People, agree to serve no more the spirit of fear,
for that spirit worships war,
and is used only to enslave the innocent.
We renounce the deceiver who deceived us with fear of each
other, and sold us out for its own selfish gain.

We, the People,
are the party of No-Defense; no war for victory or profit,
and our service to defense we call holy no more.

We, the People,
trust that our one, loving creator, has an answer to all our needs;
an answer that doesn't require murder,
or the sacrifice of <u>anyone's</u> children.

We, the Party of No-Defense,

choose as our candidate no individual figure head,

but a collective,

formed around an idea whose time has come back around,

for us to choose once again.

As a collective formed around one loving and true idea,

we are less susceptible to the corrupting temptation to seek power

for any one of us alone.


The party of No-Defense is a movement,

fueled by an idea whose purpose is to liberate all the world's

people, along with our beautiful earth,

from the war mongers' withering grip of global greed.


We, The People, are an inner-faith community,

where all are equal members,

and all equally deserve peace and security.

As a family made from our one Creator's equal Love,

our faith is rooted in trusting this Love,

and loving all whom It created equal with us.

# The Celestial Speed Up and The Great Awakening at Hand

The celestial Speed-Up and the Great

Awakening are both upon us now,

both long prophesied,

both as inevitable as Love.


The celestial speedup:

the cosmic drive to reverse humanity's backward motion.

The Great Awakening:

Love's plan for the healing of the world through us,

and its brilliant unfolding before our very own eyes.


When quiet,

you can feel the Speedup coursing through your veins,

urging you forward in the creation of the good, the

beautiful and the holy.

When your eyes are open,

you see awakening all around you,

and it never ceases to amaze you.

When your thoughts are still,

you feel drawn to something your soul remembers,

but your mind does not understand.

When your ears are clear, you hear them

both calling you by name,

to waken from your sleep of littleness,

that you might take your place among the healers of the earth.

Nor will their voices cease calling your name,

until you reply, "yes, I hear you, and yes, I will do the same".

For until you do,

your life will feel wasted on vain pursuits, senseless journeys,

and things far less valuable than bringing comfort to Love's

creations.

But to you who answer, "Yes, I will",

the lights of heaven will lay gifts of gratitude at your feet,

for it's in your shining face, they see hope of freedom,

and it's in your happy laughter,

the frightened hear Love's comforting voice.

Will you say, "I will", and step forward to accept your holy role,

Or will you put off one more day humanity's only hope?

Choose once again, you saviors of the world,

for the chance to save ourselves is come 'round again.

You are the light of the New Earth,

and the only time is now.

# *The Cosmic Plan You join,*
# *and the Love-Power You Release*

*Oh Humanity, our younger cosmic kin,*

*we know you feel inadequate against*

*the vastness of a dark and global power,*

*and a worldwide delusion.*

*For we have been at your stage of evolution before,*

*and you're a part of us we cannot abandon at such a crucial time.*

*In these precious and precarious days, Humanity,*

*pray to recognize the universe-wide support being offered you.*

*Align with us, who have heard your planet-wide cry for peace,*

*and join our purpose for happiness, health and wealth for all.*

*Let us teach you how we saved our own world,*

*from the same dark and global control that*

*strangles your world now.*

*Darling Humans,*

*you need not understand the cosmic plan you join,*

*or the love-power you release,*

*when you join your will to Love's.*

*Only know that when you do,*

*a loving power will flow through all you touch,*

*creating the good, the beautiful and the holy,*

*wherever you go and whatever you do.*

*Know that a love light will radiate through you with the power,*

*to turn hell into heaven itself.*

*Oh Humanity, our beloved own kin,*

*you are the light in this darkened world,*

*and all of heaven and humanity alike,*

*await your part in the rebirth of your radiant New Earth.*

# For The Road Ahead

Endurance, flexibility and faith;

for the road ahead cultivate these three traits.

Faith in humanity, who is your own self,

flexibility, that you might stay open to Love's directions,

and endurance to carry them out.

For the road ahead,

you have all you need, for you do not go alone,

as you go on from here with mighty companions beside you.

For the road ahead,

trust you will have all of what and whom you need,

as this path unfolds miraculously,

before each of your tentative steps.

For once you started on this road,

your safe return to the bright world from which you came,

was guaranteed in that first brave step.

For graceful passage through the twists and

turns of the road ahead,

make your mantra "fear not",

and walk only the way that Love points out,

that you may fear no evil in the night.


When tempted by despair that peace be but a dream,

let your gratitude to your teachers fill your heart,

and flood your body with the healing light of forgiveness.

# Happiness Is

"If this were different, I'd be happy,"
the lament of our perpetual discontent.

But happiness is no set of conditions,
or a thing we attain,
just like love doesn't come just because we got someone,
or something to change.

Happiness is the changeless reality we were created in and by,
the loving matrix from which all come into space and time.
Happiness is the brilliant light we all return to,
when our self-exile has exhausted its unholy reign.

Happiness is a choice for what is,
what always was,
and what always will be,
in celebration of the never-lost to an unending love.

In this holy instant now,
I choose the happiness that created me happy,
and I accept my inheritance as a creation of joy itself.

# Clear Mind, Strong Body
# for Important Days Ahead

For the important days ahead,

you midwives to the New Earth,

keep a clear mind, strong body and a vision clear of past debris.


Where once you were a sprinter,

making great starts but too poor a finish,

you must now develop the endurance of a long-distance runner;

one who has learned to pace themself for a finish line,

in a time all unknown.


You are the midwives rebirthing Humanity from fear-slaves,

to creations knowing they were created free forever.

Remember, there's nothing to fear,

as you've been training for these important times,

in this life and before.


On the mountain trails build your stamina.

On your yoga mats make your muscles limber,

and in your ecstatic dance, let your visions soar.

*Focus not on muscle gain or weight loss,*

*but only on building endurance and freedom of movement,*

*body, mind, and spirit.*

*The elements of your training,*

*as forerunners and messengers of a new day come,*

*will prepare you to be physically strong,*

*mentally clear of fear-distractions,*

*and spiritually attuned to the New Earth,*

*whose birth you're tending.*

*As midwives to the New Earth,*

*it's you who deliver the world from its*

*bondage to dark lords of fear,*

*and it's you who return the New Earth to Love's cosmic spheres.*

# Darling Humans, My Beloved Own

Darling Humans, My Beloved Own,

listen to the war drums beating in their mesmerizing tones,

drumming out patriotic hymns to the holiness of war.


As an ancient people,

we've heard these dark drummings before,

and it was always a herald of the death and destruction,

of our own people, along with our beautiful earthen home.


My beautiful and mighty companions,

remember now, if you can,

when we stood here before,

astride this familiar edge of self-annihilation.


Search your oldest memories, my dear old friends.

and remember those days when we, like now,

allowed a separated few,

to control our beautiful home into oblivion.

*Just like now,*

*I have far-memories of feeling powerless before a power,*

*global in its grasp and evil in it's goal.*

*And I have memories too, of watching*

*our beautiful garden-of-a world,*

*slip violently under dark waves never to be seen again.*

*Oh Humanity,*

*my heart weeps at the sacrifice of our beloved people,*

*who sacrifice their freedom, along with their beautiful earth,*

*for nothing that can sustain even one of us.*

*The earth does renew after eons of time,*

*and souls do return again until they learn,*

*but how many more rounds of this*

*earth-destroying children's game*

*need we play?*

*To those dark souls who crave only control,*

*war is a sacred power,*

*and they will sacrifice every last soul on their altar to death,*

*to obtain it.*

*Decide with me now, my beloved own,*

*in these precious and precarious days,*

*to join that universe-wide effort underway,*

*to reclaim Humanity from the war-monger's withering grasp,*

*and to set The New Earth free.*

# Dissolving Death together,
# by Recognizing
# the Eternal Nature of Life

The natural world,

ever-renewing and ever-providing

without conditions or exceptions,

and a stunning expression of our creator's

unending love for Its creation.


Fear,

hating life; seeks to degrade all living things,

as entropy is fear's dark calling card.


Entropy,

the supposed law of life's eventual disintegration into disorder &
decay,

is not natural to Life at all.

*Life,*

*whose eternal upwelling only gives*

*rise to more of Its own glorious expression,*

*and never sinks down to decay,*

*as only death can do.*

*Death,*

*an illusion we dissolve together,*

*by recognizing the eternal nature of life.*

# Earth Children

Earth Children,

beloved beyond your own understanding,

we, your elder spirit family,

desire to tell you of our love, care and concern for you.


You are a precious part of ourselves,

to whom we share a loving debt of family devotion.


Seek within for our voices, and learn to listen to our words,

for our voices can guide you to the safety of peace,

when the world's facades inevitably crumble down.


Through the chaos of this dissolving world,

learn to access our rendezvous place in your mind,

where we can talk and reason together.


From our beautiful meeting place deep in your mind,

we can carry you over the battlefields on fire,

and across the bridge to the worlds of Love and Light.

# Communication Is

Communication is,

and all that lives is connected by it forever.

To be in communication is the nature of life itself,

the how and why we are one.


Communication is the connecting link in the quantum web,

in which we all live,

move and have our being.


Without boundary,

communication pervades all time and space,

for creation is in constant dialogue with itself,

speaking with us as naturally,

as breath moves through our body.


Today, I retreat from the world into the quiets of nature,

to seek that sweet communication between creator and creation,

that ecstatic communion,

that does answer my every need,

real or imagined.

# Beloved Counselors in Sight

Beloved counselors in sight,

into your wise care and capable hands,

I've entrusted my own children, your spiritual siblings.

And I have full faith in you to say and do with them,

only as I have said and done with you.


Counselors to my children in sight,

you gifted your eyes to me,

that my children might see me through yours,

and for this I am grateful.

In my gratitude, I have blessed your sight,

for you reunited me with my beloved own.


All you give to me, be it your body, mind or spirit,

I will use to heal my all of my creations,

and I will do so in your name.

When thy eye is full of sight,

thy form is filled with radiant light.

Eyes given me are full of beauty and wonder.

Ears lent me are filled with beautiful music and laughter.

Mouths that form around my loving thoughts,

are gifted with speech that inspires and heals many others.

# Earth Mother

Earth Mother,

you keep my soul awake with the sights,

sounds and fragrance of your wondrous nature.

Your ancient cycles keep my mind ever-expanding,

and your beauty compels my restless mind to be still.


When Father-Spirit placed his potent and creative seed

deep into your fertile soil,

the Spirit of Creation blessed your union with the natural world,

that now feeds and heals all the children of Earth.


As stunning as your beauties are, Earth Mother,

I sense they are mere shadows of the power,

from which they all have sprung,

and to which we all belong.


Your crystalline core keeps my memory of eternal relations,

alive in my deepest center,

and does not let me forget.

*Always reminding me, Earth Mother,*

*of what you would not let me forget in time's misty vapors,*

*you call me from the world to slip back into your holy quiet,*

*to listen and to remember.*


*When reluctantly, Earth Mother,*

*I must leave your healing beauties,*

*and return to the world of bodies in time,*

*I will go singing your songs,*

*praising your earth-children and calling them back home.*


*Earth Mother,*

*your beauty is the call,*

*your quiet is the door,*

*and I, the prodigal child, am afraid of home no more.*

# *Like Every Parent Recognizes their Own Baby's Voice*

*Like every loving parent recognizes their own baby's voice,*

*I recognize your voice, my darling child.*

*I recognize the voice of every one of my creations,*

*and they recognize mine.*

*Dearest Child of My Love,*

*you wonder how I can recognize your voice*

*from all of my creations,*

*but that's nothing for an unlimited love,*

*who would not be apart from the children at Its heart.*

*Not only do I recognize the voice of each of my precious own,*

*but I am always speaking to them as any adoring parent would,*

*all through the days, and all through the nights as well.*

*What makes you a messenger for me, Dear One,*

*is not any unique trait of yours,*

*but only that when I called to you,*

*you answered me back.*

*Our talking; parent to child, child to parent,*

*is the most natural thing a soul can do,*

*and the happiest too,*

*for our talks together restore heaven to the earth again.*

# Now Is the Time

*Now is the time to summon your courage and state your mission,*

*damn the cost to your fears and all their divisions.*

*Now is the time to picture your heart's desire,*

*and resist the fears that say, "forget about it,*

*It'll never be good enough anyway".*

*Dream your happiest dreams,*

*even if you see no way to bring them to fruition.*

*For these are the days of signs and wonders,*

*where those who work for love,*

*will inherit the New Earth,*

*and be Its guide back into its awaiting cosmic family.*

# *Oneness Is My Religion,*
## *–An Ode to Our Ecstatic Dance*

Oneness is my religion,

for its idea and practice,

has made my life more like a garden of play and plenty every day.


Dancing ecstatically in this sacred space,

I remember again my heart's true devotion,

my one true religion,

the heaven that is our oneness.


Our ecstatic dance is my shaking, whirling, flying medicine,

that opens chinks in my body's armor,

and lets light stream into my wounded places.


To this dance, and to you, my Miracle-Mates,

I come to spin open my spirit-eye,

and to fling fear's grip off my heart and into the

dirt beneath my feet.

To our dance,

I come to feel what it's like in the real world,

where we know there's nothing to fear,

because we're here together as one.


The joyous noise we make here, dancing as one wild creation,

is our anthem to the oneness we are,

and it ecstatically sings" we are all one people,

and our unity makes us stronger,

than any fear that would divide us."

# Portals Back to Your Natural Mind

There are stunning patterns in the natural world,

that when meditated upon,

become codes unlocking knowledge and

releasing powers of Creation.

There are certain rhythms present in the natural world,

that when synchronized with,

carry you effortlessly down the river's

buoyant and willow-scented flow.

There are certain frequencies inherent in the natural world,

that when allowed to, can detox the body of electronic poisons

from the man-made world.

There is a hush that descends upon the mind,

as it takes in the beauties of the natural world;

a sense of quiet that is a balm to the wounds of time,

and a deep relief to man's anxious mind.

*The natural world, with all its matchless splendors,*

*is a portal back to your natural mind,*

*in all its fearless wonders.*

# Living Waters & Mind-Expanding Views

A place of warm and living waters alongside mind-expanding views,

is where whatever loves me has brought me today.

From this old porch,

perched high above a vast and mysterious valley below,

I watch storms traveling across its expansive floor,

in alternating patterns of sunset light streams,

and dark bands of rain.

As dark clouds pile up the peaks behind me,

I make myself a cup of coffee,

wrap soft wool around me,

and settle into a rocking chair for an electrifying show.

The dark and dense clouds

send electric tendrils down and over the mountain's crest,

surging through my nervous system,

and waking my own electric fields.

*What power these winds carry in their pressure differentials,*

*and how reviving they are in their static charge.*

*This storm's conductivity turns my brain circuits into a radio,*

*so I eagerly await its approach, and I listen intently.*

*Contained in the watery vapor of these enlivened winds,*

*I hear messages from ancient friends calling me by name,*

*to stand and arise as my time is nigh.*

*Riding in upon these mighty winds today,*

*I feel Great Spirit's supercharged presence,*

*and I hear its thunderous voice declaring that the time is now,*

*for there's no more time to wait.*

# So Many, for So Long

So many, for so long,

have been abused in the names of Jesus, Allah, and Avraham.

So many, for even longer, have been abused in the name of God.

But everyone on Earth, now and in times gone,

have been abused in the name of Love.


Nothing we know about these great teachers comes even close,

to what they really taught,

just like nothing we learned about love,

comes even close to what love really says and does.


For if we truly understood what these messengers taught,

and knew what love is really about,

war would be impossible,

for lack would be nothing but a dream already awakened from.

# *Prayer for My Daily Bread*

My Creator, who art in the heaven within,

perfect is Your Love,

thy loving Will be done,

on Earth as in the shining realms beyond.


I give you this day, and this precious moment too,

that I might accept my daily bread;

that manna which is your word that carries

me through all my trials,

and sustains me in all my needs, real and imagined.


Help me forgive my fearful mis-perceptions,

and all their subsequent mis-creations,

as I forgive others for theirs.


Use my hands to heal the children of Your love,

and tune my ears to hear their plaintive cry for Your loving care,

that they could see through my smiling eyes,

and feel through my loving touch.

*I am yours, as I belong to you,*

*and you are mine, as I came from you.*

# On This Side of Death and Beyond

On this side of death,

there is only wailing and mourning for a lie so cruel,

it would teach the children of eternal life,

that love and life can die.

On the other side of the belief in death,

souls sing and dance in their freedom from such a dark dream,

and the sweetest of laughter can be heard in the soft breeze,

that does whispers 'round every living thing.

Oh Humanity,

though you still suffer the fever dreams of death,

there will come a moment in time,

when you will lay down the heavy robe death wears,

to conceal its nothingness from you,

and you will gasp at the simplest truth that life ends not in death,

but ever goes on.

There and then,

Love will sweep you up in Its laughing embrace,

and wipe away the cobwebs of sleep from your now glittering eyes.

# Humanity, What Have We Done?

Why the mass shootings of our children?

Could it be only the mental illness or the guns themselves,

responsible for this terrible phenomenon?

We blame everything but our collective consent,

in our government's gross profit from massive weapon sales.


That there be no shortage in demand for our deadly product,

our government sells weapons to both sides of every conflict.


We sell implements of genocide to whoever

wants them at our price,

regardless of what children they'll be used to kill.


We claim we value our children,

but we support the endangerment of children around the world,

as we sell the bombs that kill them in their beds.


We claim we value our freedom,

but we endanger the freedoms of others all around the earth, *by the sale of weapons to corrupt governments,*

*that like ours, profit from the war industry.*


*Collectively, we've been hypnotized to support,*

*that which kills and maims children around the world,*

*and we've been programmed to feel patriotic about it.*


*And then we wonder, why so many of our **own** children,*

*are being slain by weapons of mass destruction,*

*as they sit in school or play outside.*


*So deceived were we,*

*we used our one precious vote,*

*for politicians bought and paid for by the*

*military-industrial complex,*

*who now enslave us with their security technology.*


*Our governments sold off our most precious shared possession;*

*our government for the people, and by the people,*

*and now we're but cogs in a globally corporate war machine.*


*What have we done, humanity,*

*that we should fall lower than the stones on the ground,*

*and become but slave fodder for war and taxes?*

My loving and strong people,

let us forgive ourselves for being willing slaves,

to a killing machine without a soul.


May We, the People,

use our few remaining freedoms in this world,

to choose once again,

who and what we support.

May we choose our children,

over any profit from the mass destruction,

of children of God everywhere.

# Reflected In the Natural World

My perceptions are like these wafting clouds above me,

ephemeral and quickly passing into ever-changing forms,

one moment in this form and changing in the next.

It's easy to see a whole world rising in their vaporous mists,

and to forget that world is but a misty projection.


Sometimes these clouds are dark and dense,

and bring storms that wash away my home.

Sometimes these clouds take my breath away,

with their stunning opalescence,

leaving me in a holy moment of wordless wonder.

So too, my thoughts

can be beautiful and inspiring, or dark and destroying.


This waterfall is like God's love for creation;

perpetually it flows over its brim,

into ever-filling pools of life-giving waters,

that sustain life and clean our children.

Just like God's love too,

these living waters are kept alive in their perpetual flow to us,

For God's love is constant and strengthened by our acceptance.

Reflected in the natural world,

I see the nature of my passing human perceptions,

or the splendors of Creation in Its loving will for all.

For it is my choice what I see in Its mirror of form.

# What to Remember When Your World Breaks Apart at the Seams

*Darling Ones,*

*the world has always been breaking apart at the seams,*

*for so it was made to do,*

*having been made by fear.*

*The world, as you know it now,*

*was made to tear what God made one into disconnected parts,*

*that no longer recognize each other,*

*and try to kill one another in the dark.*

*Like all illusions,*

*the world you see now will fail and fall,*

*ending in the dust from which it came.*

*Do not mourn and lament the world in its desperate state,*

*but only see it as it is, a world never true,*

*and only waiting to be seen anew.*

Raise your eyes from what is past and gone,

and look up to a world your body's eye could never find,

the world just beyond war where no fear stalks.


When it feels your world is breaking apart at the seams,

and you're tempted by doubt and fear,

be grateful, Dear Ones,

that an ancient lie is being revealed,

and can bring no more frightening dreams.


Now the seeds of good that deception did hide,

can blossom wild,

and turn your life into a garden of your happiest dreams.


Only say, "even as my world breaks apart at the seams,

I am grateful still for what Love has done for me,

and surely,

Love's plan for me must be close at hand,"


and behold,

the veil that hung heavy on your eyes, making life so dim,

will be lifted by Love's graceful hand,

revealing a life you didn't dare dream you could have.

*Remember Darling Ones, I said,*

*"Whenever you see some twisted form of the original error of fear,*

*say only, God is not fear, but love,*

*and it will soon disappear."*

# Why The Killing of Our Children En Masse?

How can it be that our children,

the heart and soul of our people,

are being targeted and murdered en masse?


Is this phenomenon simply a tragic accident of the modern world,

or are we, in any way we, en masse,

complicit in the killing of any other people's children,

en masse?


Could there be any karmic connection here that we are paying for,

with the lives of our own precious children?

One must ask these kinds of questions,

when so tragic a pattern emerges in our world.


As a nation and a people,

what have we been contributing to the world?

As a nation, we used to export our ingenuity,

and the fruits of our abundant lands.

But now, what do we give to the world,

*but bombs that kill other people's children,*

*and destroys our priceless earth.*

*How can it be that our nation's most prosperous industry,*

*is the one that builds and sells weaponry?*

*How did it come to pass that our once prosperous economy,*

*has become so morbidly obese with weapons,*

*while our children are killed by guns and our people go hungry?*

*The weapon peddlers are cunning,*

*in how they hide what their weapons do.*

*Owning the media we consume,*

*they make sure we don't see how many children,*

*their bombs kill in their beds.*

*We have sold our children's future for weapons that kill, en masse,*

*and now we wonder why **our** children are being killed by guns, en*

*masse.*

# Why Our Children Suffer the Same

If it's true, that everything happening **to** our people,

reflects what is happening **within** our people,

then what is the gun violence epidemic reflecting from the inside

of us?

If violence to children,

is happening in our country at such an alarming rate,

what kind of violence have we been perpetrating, as a country,

to the children of other countries,

that we'd rather not see?

The violence our government projects across the globe,

killing innnocents abroad,

has returned, like demonic spawn,

to us, it's source.

War mongers, kept cold and starving

by their lord and master, fear,

long for violence in the secret places of their heart,

and they call war holy and patriotic,

that we'll sacrifice our children for the wars **they** want.


The brokers of war know our willingness to sell our soul,

for a pocket full of treasure, and a belly full of pride,

so they tempt us with trifling treasures and vain pursuits.

They use fear and hate,

that we might sell our sovereignty, individual and collective,

to a war machine whose only fuel is our children's death.


Although it was manufactured,

we consented to violence waged around the world in our name,

and now we wonder why our children do suffer violence the same.

# The Silence Freed Up in
# Me When the Grid Went Down

As the electrical grid went down around me today,

I encountered something within me,

that had been waiting on me to be quiet enough to hear it.


As the cloud of worldly frequency subsided,

my inner eye blinked open, and my inner ear cleared.

I then heard a quiet voice within me that compelled me,

and I had a vision that woke me from a spell I'd been under.


"Welcome back to now, dear one,"

a voice said, with a twinkle in its tone,

how much we delight in our talks with you, you cannot guess.


It is our sweetest pleasure to share with you cosmic visions,

and liberating truths,

but they are oft drowned out by too many electromagnetic fields;

man-made fields meant to dull your inner senses,

and fence in your mind with fear's limitations.

You have become addicted to external sensory input,

*but only what comes from within you can truly satisfy a soul.*

*There's never a time we're not offering you our thoughts;*

*no time we're not reminding you to go inward and upward,*

*that you might know realms of beauty and peace,*

*you cannot even imagine yet.*

*But there are so few moments your senses are not plugged already,*

*by stimuli from without,*

*preventing you from feeling our presence and hearing our words.*

*Use the calming sounds of the natural world,*

*to detox your brain and quiet your mind,*

*that your inner senses may reawaken,*

*and bring your capacity for true perception back online.*

*The world seeks to hypnotize you with its low-vibration hum,*

*but the signal from Source,*

*will never stop drawing your attention to the real world,*

*the sight of which begins within your own quiet mind.*

*Do not fear the lower realms,*

*with their dark intent to entrap and mine all souls.*

*You need but attune your thoughts to Love's universal tones,*

*and no invisible, dark frequency bands,*

*can bind your mind or tie your hands any longer".*

# Who Controls the Strings?

Who is controlling the strings by which we dance so unconsciously?

Who are the shrouded few who use us for their selfish agendas?

Whoever they are, and from wherever they operate,

they are still but projections of our self-hate;

projections we disowned,

that now hate us for rejecting them.

Just who is it that's trying to kill us off,

as useless eaters to them?

Whom could they be,

but the projections of our own belief that we don't deserve to live,

projected on the world and fed by our fears.

To that which wants me dead,

I say, "You are but my own belief,

and I cannot be killed".

Take heed light workers,

keep your bodies strong,

*and your mind clear of petty thoughts that drain your life force,*

*for the liberation at hand, you will need them both.*


*Remember, **we** are the strong ones in this spiritual war,*

*because we are united in love, and they are not.*

*The shrouded ones are weak,*

*for no one can unite around fear that only divides.*


***We** are a unity of equals in Creation's love,*

*and in reality,*

*we are always free from fear's control,*

*for we are real and fear is not.*

# The Practice of Silence

In the practice of silence,

your mind is quiet, and judgment laid aside,

allowing your inner eye to see a beauty in the world,

not seen before by your human eyes.

Gazing deeply into the beauties of nature,

one finds a spotless mirror revealing the grandeur,

living in the unearthed recesses of one's own mind.

There are no depths to which the practice of silence cannot reach,

no answer to any need this practice won't lay at your feet.

For in the quiet and beautiful here and now,

wherein stillness and beauty reign supreme,

your loving Creator is waiting to be with you,

and end your lonely dream.

# Praying For the World

Warmly ensconced in fire-warmth and soft wool,

heavy snows blanket this mountain in deep sky-powder sublime,

and I am transfixed by firelight.


Finally free enough from the world's persistent pull,

I let lose the world's fearful hold,

and I let peace take control,

mind and heart, body and soul.


That's when I feel humanity's call.


I have always gone to mountain tops to pray for humanity's sake,

and tonight is no exception.

From here,

high above the battleground, where fear wages its endless wars,

the world looks only like children needing love,

and not a hell I must avoid.

From this holy place on high tonight,

I pray for humanity to re-member itself as innocent and whole,

and never in need of anything through war.


Here by the fire,

lit and warm on this deep snow night,

I wish for all creation the safety and comfort that is Creator's delight,

for all Its creations,

Winter, Spring, day or night.

# Storm Watchers and Brave Sentinels Alike

Storm watchers and brave sentinels alike,

you who gaze into distant horizons for humanity's sake,

what do you do,

when you see a storm approaching in the misty distance?

Do you hide what you saw to avoid being hated by the fearful,

or do you ask Love to prepare you and others,

for its sure arrival?

If invited,

Love will prepare you such that you will have what you need,

when you need it,

and so will the others Love sends you.

Though it be a risk to inform the sleeping and the numb,

of what they do not want to come,

don't forget,

they are protected who protect God's own,

which is everyone.

And what of those who know you've seen true, Storm Watchers,

but believe they can't prepare as you?

Are they correct,

or is there something everyone can do,

to help themselves and others,

to weather whatever storms may come?


Brave sentinels, tell them true,

of the Love that's forgotten no one,

and who is their most sure protection,

whatever may come.


Storm Watchers and Brave Sentinels alike,

hold steady, hold strong,

be firmly rooted in Love's certain outcome,

and do as you are guided by the Spirit,

who tends us all as one.

# The Path Back to Peace

The path back to peace winds gently beside life-giving waters,

and is so delicately dappled in sunlight,

that your eyes are delighted,

and your senses come to life as you walk it.


The path back to peace is clear,

as it winds through aromatic woods,

with no long-dead branches reaching out to ensnare you.

For as divinely beautiful as this path is,

that is how safe it is as well.


When the weary traveler is overheated

from the intensity of the world,

the path back to peace is shaded with artfully hung greenery.


When the peace-pilgrim is chilled by an uncaring world,

the path back is flooded by the warming radiance of the rising sun.

The path back to peace is a well-lit, safe and inspiring path;

a path that compels you to follow it with a joy you never knew,

and a peace that passes your understanding.


One finds their unique path back to peace,

when it is but peace they desire for themselves and all others.


What more holy of a gift can one give to the world,

then to find one's own path back to peace,

and to walk happily upon it?

# Stepping Lightly Over Lifeless Shells

The rot in my gut is the dead-matter left behind,

after my too quickly passing pleasures faded away,

leaving me bloated but craving more.


The fatty bulge around my core,

is witness to my false belief I don't have enough right now,

and must need more.


The detritus of my addictions clog my core with a heaviness,

and robs me of my desire to dance like the free child I used to be.

The sad, cruel voice of my many demanding needs,

tells me I'll never be innocent again,

never light enough to laugh and play again,

as a radiant child without sin.


My addiction to passing pleasures that end in pain,

are but my weak substitutions,

for the lasting joys I found seeking deeply in my own mind,

and looking into the universe in another's eyes.

The only lasting joys I've known,

are the ones I never found in the world,

but only in something eternal in me,

and in helping others to find their own.


The pleasures of healing,

and being a friend to the world,

are pleasures that do not pass quickly away,

and they cost nothing in their wake.


My imposter self,

cloaked in the fleshy folds of my body,

seeks only passing pleasures,

and to avoid their inevitable pains.

Where my true self offers me only joys that last,

and gifts that offer only gain.


Now, on the sacred grounds of this precious life of mine,

I step lightly over the lifeless shells of my many pleasure-pains,

and I make my way back to the innocent child I remain,

that has never stopped calling my name.

# All That was Hidden

Once jealously guarded by dark ones who serve only themselves,

universal truths are being revealed again in plain sight,

for all to see with their own open eyes.


Never has truth been hidden,

only feared and distorted,

but ever held in safekeeping,

until anyone seeks its plain face.

For truly,

no one can fail who seeks to find the Truth where it waits for them,

quietly within their own innocent self.


Learn to enter deeply into the silences of your own mind.

Go find what you hid there in shame's shadow,

that you might bring it into the full light of Love's unending care.


Fear not to look within, Dear Children of the Light,

for Love offers Its strength to face what we've hidden;

our fear and our holiness, alike,

and vision clear enough to know we've been forgiven.

But do know, Glorious Children of a Glorious Creator,

the moment your will becomes one with the Loving Will of Creation,

the storehouse doors of an infinite universe fly open,

bringing you everything you need to take your place,

among the healers of a world in such pain.

# Oh Love, What Do You Do?

Oh Love,

What would you do if you were witnessing the genocide of a people,

livestreaming on the screen in your hand?

Tell me now,

that I might respond the same.


What do you see, Love,

when you look upon the slaughter of your own beautiful children,

every one of whom I know you adore?

Tell me true,

for the way I'm seeing it fills me with pain and rage;

two emotions I know fuel the fires of my hate.


Dear one,

Have you not seen me working through many souls over time,

resisting not evil,

but dispelling dark forces with naught but the simple truth?

*Resist not evil with your hate,*

*but only speak forth the truth,*

*that all souls were created equal in their inalienable rights,*

*to life, love, and freedom from want.*

*And do not stop speaking this truth,*

*until all the slaves are free everywhere.*

*It requires no hate to simply say, "No, not in my name."*

*And remember too, brave child of mine,*

*how the evil agendas of the few,*

*that loom so large and oppressive over the many,*

*do fall like the walls of Jericho,*

*at the joyous sounds the many do make,*

*when they stand as one in this simple truth.*

# Vietnam Talks Again

Here we are again, as a country, and a people,

having the Vietnam talks again.

It's the age-old conversation we have between the old

and the young when war looms large on the horizon.

It's a dialogue between the elders, who sacrificed for their country,

and the youth, who see how immoral and murderous,

their own government has become.

Our patriotic elders say,

"We laid our lives on the line for the country,

you're now protesting against,

and the corruption you speak of, must be a mad conspiracy."

Our idealistic youth reply,

"With all due respect brave elders,

the country for which you laid your life on the line,

has been co-opted and captured by an immoral force,

which is now being used against you, and every free soul.

You do not see it because you do not want to see,

how cruelly you've been used,

by a country you bravely offered your life to protect.


History is full of governments that started with virtuous intent,

but became corrupt in the hands of a few,

who sought to possess power for themselves.

Yet it is still soul-shocking when it happens to yours."

9 798218 354480